LEVELED POEMS

for Small-Group Reading Lessons

40 Reproducible Poems With Mini-Lessons for Guided Reading Levels E–N

PAMELA CHANKO

New York • Toronto • London • Auckland • Sydney
Mexico City • New Delhi • Hong Kong • Buenos Aires

"But Then" from *Up the Windy Hill* by Aileen Fisher, copyright © 1953, 1981 Aileen Fisher.
Used by permission of Marian Reiner on behalf of the Boulder Public Library Foundation, Inc.
All other poems in this collection used by permission of Scholastic Inc.

ISBN: 978-0-545-59363-2

Cover design by Michelle H. Kim
Interior design by Grafica
Illustration by Kelly Kennedy
Copyright © 2014 by Pamela Chanko
Published by Scholastic Inc. All rights reserved.
Printed in the U.S.A.
First printing, January 2014.

5 6 7 8 9 10   40   21 20 19 18 17 16

Table of Contents

The Poems

Introduction

Welcome to *Leveled Poems for Small-Group Reading Lessons*—a brand new way of using leveled text in the classroom! Teachers have long been provided with leveled readers, books, passages, and so on—but why should leveled text be limited to prose? Poetry is a form of text (and of art!) that should be accessible to all students. Plus, the one-page, doubled-sided format of the poems in this collection can make the text less intimidating and more appealing to all readers, from the struggling to the high-achieving. Most of the poems rhyme as well, adding an element of fun—and helpful predictability—to the text.

Each poem is laid out like a reproducible "card"—the illustrated poem begins on the front and continues on the back, followed by engaging "Read and Think" questions to assess comprehension. Simply make a two-sided photocopy of each poem and you're ready to go. (TIP: For added durability, use card stock and/or laminate.) You'll find four poems each at levels E–N—making for a whopping 40 poems in all! The poems are perfect for small-group reading lessons, but can also be used for independent work, take-home activities, or even whole-class reading and discussion.

Leveled Text in the Age of Common Core

The Common Core Standards require that all students move up a staircase of text complexity, reading more and more challenging texts as the school year goes on. The standards also suggest that in order to get all students reading at end-of-year levels, teachers must provide careful, effective scaffolding to those who need it. Using leveled text in small-group reading lessons helps teachers accomplish just that! Explicit instruction in comprehension and fluency with texts that are increasingly challenging to students is the very goal of the leveled reading model.

Another focus of the Common Core is close reading—careful attention to text that involves critical thinking and deeper levels of comprehension and evaluation. Lessons structured using the guided reading model provide the perfect environment for meeting this goal. In addition, leveled text plays an important role in students' independent reading. The Common Core states that students must have access to many different levels of text, including those at their own reading level as well as those that are more challenging.

Why Use Poetry?

Poetry is unique in that it is inherently complex text—it's a genre that teaches students to look at language differently and, often, to learn new rules (such as beginning each line with a capital letter, line breaks in the middle of sentences, and so on). Reading poetry requires students to learn flexibility of language depending on its form—a highly sophisticated concept. In addition, poetry is an art form that expresses ideas in a limited space. This makes it perfect for encouraging higher-order thinking about text, and for deepening understanding of vocabulary and the beauty of language itself.

So get ready to introduce students to the magical world of poetry—a whole new way to inspire a love and appreciation of language and reading!

Using the Poems

Following, you'll find great tips for helping students get the most out of these poems during small-group reading lessons. Of course, as their teacher, you know best what kind of support your students need; but these general guidelines are helpful to keep in mind.

Before Reading

The amount of scaffolding you provide before students dive into the text depends on the subject matter of the poem and the text's level of challenge for the group you're working with. If students do require scaffolding, here are some pre-reading activities that can help.

Context: Some poems in this collection (such as "Abe Lincoln Grows Up" and "In the Rainforest") are based on content-area information from social studies and science. You might like to give students background, or review what they know, before reading these works. For instance, you might discuss the basics of the civil rights movement, and Martin Luther King's role, before reading "Following Martin."

Vocabulary: Depending on students' decoding and word-interpretation skills, you might like to introduce any general academic (Tier 2) vocabulary or content-area (Tier 3) vocabulary. Words like *scenery* ("A Question of Rhyme") and *tapir* ("In the Rainforest") might be introduced before reading to increase fluency during reading.

Strategy: Again, depending on the difficulty of the text relative to your group's reading level, you might like to introduce and pre-teach a special strategy or purpose for students to keep in mind as they read. You can get ideas from the mini-lessons (pages 9–16), or choose a general reading strategy, such as looking for causes and effects, finding the main idea or "gist" in each stanza, and so on. (For some groups it may be better to focus on simply reading the poem straight through first, and trying a strategy on a subsequent reading.)

During Reading

As you read a poem with students, focus on multiple skills: decoding, fluency, comprehension, and close reading. You can do this by reading the poem multiple times, delving deeper and deeper into the text with each reading. Here are examples of some routines you might use.

First Reading: Have students read the poem softly to themselves as you listen in. Pay attention to challenges they encounter and how they deal with those challenges. For instance, if students stumble over a word, do they go back and self-correct, or ask for help if necessary? Can you hear students using phonics skills to "sound-out" unfamiliar words? Are students using other print-awareness strategies, such as tracking print with a finger? As you listen in, provide scaffolding to students as needed or requested.

Second Reading: Once students know how to pronounce all the words in the poem, focus on the special kind of fluency that poetry requires: reading with rhythm and meter. You might model reading the poem aloud and have students echo you after each line or try a choral reading. This helps students enjoy the feeling and sound of the language, an essential component of poetry.

Third Reading: This time, focus on comprehension and critical thinking. On the back of each poem sheet you'll find two text-based comprehension questions and one "stretch" question. Answers to the first two questions can be found directly in the text of the poem, so they provide good insight into students' basic understanding. The third question involves careful, close reading and use of critical thinking skills. You will find questions that require students to make inferences, interpret vocabulary, connect the text to illustrations, and so on. Many of these questions ask students to find evidence in the poem's text to back up their answers. They also encourage discussion among students as each student responds and comments on others' responses. During these discussions, invite students to ask their own questions about anything they may need help understanding or clarifying.

Additional Readings: Use the poem to model and teach a specific comprehension strategy, as suggested in the "Before Reading" section. Depending on students' skill level, you might use the gradual-release method: First, model using the strategy yourself with a think-aloud. For example, with "Stanley the Scaredy-Shark," you might focus on main idea and details and say: "This first stanza tells me that Stanley is afraid of life in the ocean. It tells me what the main character is like." Next, work on the strategy along with students, for example, ask: "What information can you find in the next few stanzas? Read a few examples of things Stanley is scared of. These are details." Finally, have students try the strategy on their own, using the last two stanzas. Ask: "What is the big idea, or main event? What are some details about how it happened?"

After Reading

There are so many ways to extend the reading of a poem that you will doubtless come up with lots of activities of your own. Here are just a few suggestions!

Mini-Lessons: On pages 9–16 of this guide, you'll find quick and easy mini-lessons to follow up each poem in the collection. The lessons help you home in on a variety of essential foundational skills, such as phonological awareness, phonics, spelling, vocabulary, and fluency. You'll also find lessons related to the art form of poetry itself: rhythm, rhyme, figurative language, alliteration, and so on.

Writing: Writing about reading is an important skill that students will need to use more and more as they move up the grades. While many of the provided mini-lessons have embedded writing activities within them, you can have students write about any poem. Ask them to evaluate the piece and give reasons why they did or did not enjoy it; write a different poem, or a narrative, on the same topic; answer one of the Read and Think questions on the sheet in writing; or write to compare two different poems. The possibilities are virtually endless!

Illustrating: While each poem in this collection is illustrated, students can still draw their own pictures to represent a poem. They can use drawings to express the content or create abstract patterns as they listen to you read the poem aloud, following your rhythm and expression.

Recording: Invite students to make recordings of themselves reading the poem aloud. Students can do this individually, in pairs, or as a group. Place the recordings in a listening center for independent read-along work.

Meeting the Common Core State Standards

The activities in this book will help you meet your specific state language arts standards as well as those recommended by the Common Core State Standards Initiative (CCSSI). The activities support students in meeting standards in the following strands for grades 1–3: Reading Literature; Reading Foundational Skills; Writing; Speaking and Listening; and Language.

The abbreviated standards listed below (for more details on the standards, go to the CCSSI Web site at www.corestandards.org) indicate skills explicitly taught and/or called out in the lesson plans provided in this book. Keep in mind, however, that many additional skills indicated in the standards will be addressed naturally as students read the poems and do the extension activities.

<table>
<tr><th colspan="5" style="text-align:center">GRADE</th></tr>
<tr><th rowspan="2">STRAND</th><th></th><th>Grade 1</th><th>Grade 2</th><th>Grade 3</th></tr>
<tr>
<td>Reading Literature</td>
<td>RL 1.1
RL 1.4
RL 1.10</td>
<td>RL 2.1
RL 2.4
RL 2.7
RL 2.10</td>
<td>RL 3.1
RL 3.4
RL 3.5
RL 3.7</td>
</tr>
<tr>
<td>Reading Foundational Skills</td>
<td>RF 1.1a
RF 1.2a, 1.2b
RF 1.3a, 1.3b, 1.3c, 1.3e, 1.3g
RF 1.4a, 1.4b, 1.4c</td>
<td>RF 2.3a, 2.3b, 2.3c, 2.3d, 2.3e, 2.3f
RF 2.4a, 2.4b, 2.4c</td>
<td>RF 3.3a, 3.3c, 3.3d
RF 3.4a, 3.4b, 3.4c</td>
</tr>
<tr>
<td>Writing</td>
<td>W 1.5
W 1.8</td>
<td>W 2.1
W 2.5
W 2.7
W 2.8</td>
<td>W 3.1b
W 3.4
W 3.7
W 3.10</td>
</tr>
<tr>
<td>Speaking and Listening</td>
<td>SL 1.1a, 1.1b, 1.1c
SL 1.2
SL 1.3
SL 1.4
SL 1.5
SL 1.6</td>
<td>SL 2.1a, 2.1b, 2.1c
SL 2.2
SL 2.3
SL 2.5
SL 2.6</td>
<td>SL 3.1a, 3.1b, 3.1c, 3.1d
SL 3.2
SL 3.3
SL 3.5
SL 3.6</td>
</tr>
<tr>
<td>Language</td>
<td>L 1.1b, 1.1f
L 1.2d
L 1.4a, 1.4b
L 1.5c
L 1.6</td>
<td>L 2.1e
L 2.2c
L 2.3a
L 2.4a
L2.5a, 2.5b
L2.6</td>
<td>L 3.1a
L 3.2e, 3.2f
L 3.3a, 3.3b
L 3.4a
L 3.5a, 3.5b
L 3.6</td>
</tr>
</table>

Assessment

As students read the poems, you can use the rubric below to assess a variety of developing skills over time. This record, along with your own personal observations, can help you determine when students are ready to move to the next guided reading level.

Reading Skills Checklist										
Name										
Date										
Decoding and Fluency **Does the student…**										
use sound-spelling relationships to decode unfamiliar words?										
self-correct by rereading to pronounce words?										
use appropriate inflections to read with expression?										
read with appropriate rate on successive readings?										
Vocabulary **Does the student…**										
use surrounding text to figure out meanings of new words?										
use illustrations to help determine word meanings?										
understand and use new vocabulary in other contexts?										
understand word nuances and relationships between words?										
Comprehension **Does the student…**										
ask questions to confirm or clarify understanding?										
answer simple text-based questions correctly?										
use critical thinking skills and experience to make inferences?										
cite evidence from the text to back up answers and opinions?										

Poem-by-Poem Mini-Lessons

While each poem in this collection is rich with opportunities for study in a variety of areas, the mini-lessons that follow provide you with quick and easy suggestions to capitalize on specific skills that arise naturally from each work.

Mix a Pancake   Level E

This poem is great for a quick lesson on short and long vowel sounds. Read the word *pancake* aloud, separating each syllable. Ask, "Which syllable has the short *a* sound?" (*first*) "Which has the long *a* sound?" (*second*) Then extend the activity by going for a short- and long-vowel hunt through the rest of the poem. Words with short vowels include *mix, pop, it, in, pan, toss, catch,* and *can*; words with long vowels include *fry* and *you*.

There Was an Old Woman   Level E

In verses such as this one, rhythm and rhyme can be more important than the words themselves. The way the poem *sounds* is often more important than what it *says*. Demonstrate this concept by substituting a few words with new ones, such as *old woman* and *pie*. Then you can make up a silly line to end the verse. Here's an example: *There was a young farmer/I heard someone tell/He went to sell fruit/But his fruit would not sell./ The farmer went home/But the step was too high/He tripped and he fell/And his fruit went "bye-bye"!*

Six Little Ducks   Level E

Use this poem to focus on animal sounds and rhyming words. Point out the word *quack* and ask, "What other animal sounds do you know? What noise does a pig make?" (*oink*) "How about a sheep?" (*baa*) Finally, ask, "What animal makes a sound that rhymes with the words *knew* and *too*?" (*cow; moo*) Then you can make up your own poem about six little *cows* that you once knew, where one leads the others with a "*Moo, moo, moo!*"

I Love Apples!   Level E

This is a great poem for practicing an important element of fluency—reading with expression. First, invite students to find all the exclamation points in the poem (there are four). Ask, "When a sentence ends with an exclamation point, how should you read it?" (*in a happy, excited way*) Next, point out that the last word in the poem is printed in all capital letters. Often, this means that the reader should say that word in a louder voice. Practice reading the poem a few times, encouraging students to show their exuberance!

What Is Summer?   Level F

With this poem, take an opportunity to teach students about parts of speech as well as the craft of poetry. Explain that usually only adjectives can be used to describe things, for instance, "Summer is warm." In poetry, however, it's okay to use language in unusual ways. In most of this poem, *summer*, a noun, is described using other nouns! Try it out with a shared writing activity. Choose a subject, such as school, and describe it with nouns, for instance: *school is pencils; school is friends*; or even *school is homework*!

Clouds   Level F

Explore figurative language and metaphor with this poem. Explain that a metaphor compares two things by substituting one for the other. Metaphors help create pictures in our heads. Discuss how "white sheep" stand for clouds (*both are white and fluffy*) and a "blue hill" stands for the sky (*both are blue and high up*). This makes the poem sound much more interesting than if the poet just called things by their real names! Brainstorm metaphors for other things in nature by thinking about what they look, sound, or feel like. For instance, you might call thunder a *lion's roar* or trees *stalks of celery*!

Crayons   Level F

This poem is perfect for a phonics lesson on *r*-blends. Point out the *cr* in the title and have students pronounce each sound, then blend them together. Next, read the whole word aloud. Do the same for the other two *r*-blend words in the poem: *friend* and *broke*. Reinforce these phonemes with an *r*-blend chart. Create three columns headed *cr, fr,* and *br.* Begin by writing the words from the poem in the appropriate columns. (You might like to use a different color marker for the first two letters.) Then, brainstorm more words for each column, such as *crack, crown, cry, crab; fry, free, frog, fruit;* and *broom, brick, brown, branch.*

But Then   Level F

Use this poem for spelling practice with hyphens. Explain that hyphens can be used to break up a word at the end of a line if there is not enough room to finish it. Point out the word *something* in the second stanza, and show students how the word begins at the end of one line and ends at the beginning of the next. Then explain that words must be broken after a complete syllable. Demonstrate the reason by writing *so–mething* on the board. If the word were

broken up that way, it would be much more difficult to read correctly! Write a list of two-syllable words and invite students to tell where they should be broken. Then draw a line between the word parts.

The Child in the Mirror   Level G

Expand on the text of this poem by introducing sophisticated vocabulary and exploring word relationships and nuances. Begin by pointing out the word *funny.* Together, brainstorm other words that relate to *funny,* such as *hilarious* and *wacky.* Then discuss the slight differences between the words by giving examples: a *funny* person might tell a joke; a *hilarious* person might be the class clown; and a *wacky* person might do something a little crazy, like coming to school in pajamas! You can do the same with the words *smart* (*brainy, wise*) and *friendly* (*kind, outgoing*).

If You Smile at a Crocodile   Level G

This poem is terrific for teaching and reviewing the magic *e*! Point out that the words *smile* and *crocodile* each have an *e* at the end. This makes the vowel sound a long *i.* Then point to the word *bite.* Ask, "What would this word be if we took away the magic *e*?" (*bit*) Do the experiment with more long *i* words (*fin/fine, dim/dime*) as well as long *a* words (*can/cane, tap/tape*) and long *o* words (*hop/hope, rob/robe*).

Snowman Song   Level G

This is a good poem for teaching repetition. Go over the text with students, looking at how many times the word *sun* is used. Explain that many poems use repetition to make the language sound musical—and make the poems easy to remember! Together, brainstorm nursery rhymes that use the same technique, for instance: <u>*Humpty Dumpty*</u> *sat on a wall/* <u>*Humpty Dumpty*</u> *had a great fall/* <u>*All the king's*</u> *horses/ And* <u>*all the king's*</u> *men....* Another example is <u>*Pat-a-cake, Pat-a-cake,*</u> *baker's man/ Bake me a* <u>*cake*</u> *as fast as you can...* And of course, don't forget "This Little Piggy Went to Market," which begins each line with the same three words!

The Wind   Level G

Focus on the end of the poem, having students read aloud what the wind "says." Explain that *whoosh* is a word that imitates a sound—in this case, the sound of the wind. Give a few more examples of words that imitate sounds, such as *clang* (school bell), *buzz* (bee), and *crack* (egg breaking). Then introduce the word *onomatopoeia*. It's a technique many poets use to make the sounds in their poems come to life! Together, make a list of other onomatopoeic words, along with things that make the sounds. Note that some sounds can come from more than one thing! Examples are: *munch* (eating) *click* (computer mouse, keyboard, camera), *fizz* (bubbly drink), *boom* (thunder, fireworks), and *hiss* (snake, cat).

Once There Was a Little Frog   Level H

This poem is slightly unusual in that it contains dialogue. That makes it perfect for teaching an important element of punctuation—quotation marks. Point out the first set of quotation marks (in the fourth line) and ask, "Who is saying these words?" (*the little frog*) Then point out the second set of quotation marks (in the seventh line of the poem) and ask the same question. (*the little flea*) Explain that quotation marks tell when someone is speaking. They surround the words that the speaker says. You can also introduce the comma rule: a comma is always placed after the "speaking" word (*says, answers, replies,* etc.) and before the dialogue. For practice, you might have volunteers say sentences aloud and then transcribe them onto the board, using correct punctuation.

The Forgotten Acorn   Level H

Use this poem to focus on different vowel spellings and vowel pairs. Point out that the words *deep* and *tree* both have the long *e* sound, and spell it with *ee*. Next, show students that the words *bury* and *very* spell the same long *e* sound with a *y*. Come up with more words for each spelling pattern, such as *bee, green, happy,* and *many*. Then do a similar activity for words with the long *o* sound: in the poem you will find *grow, know,* and *oak*. Some additional long *o* words with these spelling patterns are *show, glow, boat,* and *coat*.

Amazing Changes   Level H

This poem is great for practicing fluency with end punctuation. Point out lines of the poem that end with a question mark, an exclamation point, and a period. Model reading the different lines aloud, showing students how your voice goes up at a question mark, sounds excited at an exclamation point, and stays level at a period. Invite volunteers to practice reading each type of line, mimicking your inflections.

Days of Adventures   Level H

Focus this mini-lesson on making connections between illustrations and text. Reread the first part of the poem and invite students to describe the illustrations on the front. Then, turn the page over, again reading the text and asking students to describe the pictures. Next, ask, "How do the illustrations help show the poem's twist ending? How does the picture on the back of the page show events differently than the front?" (Lead students to see that the illustration on the back reveals that the events are coming from a book, which is helping the child imagine that they are real.)

A Pet Needs a Vet   Level I

This poem is perfect for a lesson on word play with homophones. First, explain that homophones are words that sound the same, but are spelled differently and mean different things. Write out a few examples, such as *flower/flour, write/right, son/sun,* and *eight/ate.* Look at the words together, examining their spellings and discussing their meanings. Then explain that sometimes poets use homophones to make a joke. Point to the seventh line of the poem and ask, "What is a word that sounds like *hoarse* but means something else?" (*horse*) "Why would a pony feeling *hoarse* be funny?" (*A pony always feels like a horse, because it is one!*)

My Tree and Me   Level I

This poem is perfect for teaching apostrophes. Explain that apostrophes can either be used to show possession (*Pete's book, Mom's briefcase*) or to create a contraction. A contraction is when one or more letters in a word are replaced by an apostrophe. Often, contractions tie two words together. Go over each contraction in the poem by reading the word, saying what it means, and naming the letter that's left out: *it's* (*it is, i*) ; *spring's* (*spring is, i*),

doesn't (*does not; o*) and 'round (*around, a*). Then work together to brainstorm more contractions, such as *can't, don't, weren't,* and *aren't.* You might write each word without the apostrophe and have students tell you where it should be placed.

Winter Dress-Up   Level I

Use this poem to teach compound words. Begin by pointing out the word *snowman.* Ask: "What two small words do you see in this big word?" (*snow, man*) Explain that compound words join two separate words together, which helps give a clue to the word's meaning. A *snowman* is a *man* made out of *snow!* Find other compound words in the poem, such as *snowsuit* and *waterproof.* Then brainstorm more compound words that contain these word parts—you can even mix and match! (Examples: *snowflake, snowstorm, waterfall, fireman, fireproof*).

Giant Dinosaurs   Level I

Focus on the many adjectives in this poem to help write your own! First, point out words that describe the dinosaurs, such as *giant, angry,* and *playful.* Then tell students that there is a kind of poem that contains only adjectives! Show students what an acrostic is by writing the word *DINOSAURS* vertically down the left side of a sheet of chart paper. Then explain that each line should be an adjective that describes the topic, beginning with that letter. Complete the acrostic with the group, using words such as *Dazzling, Interesting, Noisy,* and *Old!*

Garden Goodies   Level J

Use this poem to focus on suffixes. Point out the words that end with the suffix -ful: wonderful and beautiful. Explain that a suffix is a word part that goes at the end of a word, and that different suffixes have different meanings: -ful, for example, usually means "full of." Write the word wonderful and draw a line after wonder. Then ask, "Putting these two word parts together, what do you think this word means?" (full of wonder) Then do the same for beautiful (full of beauty). Together, list more words that end with -ful and dissect their meanings, for example, colorful (full of color), hopeful (full of hope), and fearful (full of fear).

Stormy Weather   Level J

Use this poem to focus on sensory details. Together, find parts of the poem that appeal to the senses. For instance, there is the sound of the rain (pitter-pat, splatter), the feeling of the puddle (muddy, wet) and the sight of raindrops dancing. Show students how these kinds of details can help them experience the poem, rather than just read it. Then try coming up with your own sensory details for a different kind of weather, for instance, snow. You can see snowflakes flutter, feel the cold flakes landing on your tongue, hear people stomping through the snow, and so on.

Mamas and Babies   Level J

Some baby animal names may be challenging to students. You can teach content vocabulary using visuals as context clues. Ask, "What is a joey? Whose baby is it? Point to the joey in the picture." The text connects joeys to kangaroos, which students are likely to recognize; they can then easily find the joey in its mother's pocket! Use a similar procedure for the words pups, hatchlings, foals, and kits. You might even do research on interesting animal baby names (for example, otter/whelp, platypus/puggle). Then write and illustrate your own poem! (The poem need not rhyme, but you might use a similar text structure: Mama ____s have ___s.)

Spring Messages   Level J

This poem is full of action words, or verbs, making it ideal for teaching adverbs. First, show students how some of the nouns are described by adjectives (mighty crow, tiny peep), but none of the verbs are described. Challenge students to expand the lines of the poem by adding adverbs, for example: the robin began to sing softly; the rabbit hopped quickly and thumped his feet loudly. Explain that adverbs commonly describe how something is done. Add that sometimes a phrase can act like an adverb and tell where, when or why: The rabbit hopped on the grass and into its hole.

Whale Song   Level K

Focus this lesson on the poem's unusual rhyme scheme. First, explain how a poem's rhyme scheme is marked: the end of each line is labeled with a letter, starting from the beginning of the alphabet. The same letters are used for lines that rhyme, while the next letter is used for each new sound. Give an example of a simple ABCB rhyme, such as: My puppy dog/Is very sweet/She always begs/For a treat. Then turn to "Whale Song," showing students that the first stanza is AAB. Then work together to figure out the second stanza: CCB. For a real challenge, try marking the third stanza: DEFEEF!

Bare Feet and Dog   Level K

Use this poem to demonstrate how sound devices can bring out emotion. First, point out how the word feet appears at the end of many lines (repetition). Then point out that the poem ends with an AABB rhyme. Using different techniques in one poem provides contrast, and leads the reader through different feelings. While every reader will have a personal response, you can offer this sample interpretation: the emphasis on the word *feet*, along with the short length of those lines, imitates the movement of a dog running here and there, always underfoot and in the way. But when the poem shifts to a lilting rhyme, it shows how much affection the poet has for her dog, no matter what the dog does!

Counting Sheep   Level K

This poem is great for teaching word families. The poem includes three of the most common families: *-eep*, *-ight*, and *–ore*. Start by creating a three-column chart, heading each column with a word family. Begin each column with the two words from the poem: *sleep, sheep; light, tight;* and *more, snore*. Then work together to brainstorm more words for each column, for example: *beep, deep, jeep, keep; might, fight, right, sight;* and *sore, tore, chore, score.* Then try using the words to make up silly sentences, or a class poem!

Abe Lincoln Grows Up   Level K

Use this poem to practice irregular spellings with silent letters. Since there are no real "rules" for these spellings, students need as much exposure to the words as possible. Point out that both *honest* (silent *h*) and *write* (silent *w*) appear twice in the poem. Explain that the silent letter does not always come in the beginning of the word; it is sometimes in the middle or end. Then list more silent-*h* and silent-*w* words, such as *hour, ghost, rhyme, through, hurrah, wrinkle, wrist, wrong, awry* and *sword*. Read the words aloud several times with students, and keep the lists up for future reference. You might also take this opportunity to study silent-*k* words (*knee, know, knit*) and silent-*b* words (*comb, crumb, lamb*).

Stanley the Scaredy-Shark   Level L

This poem is perfect for teaching alliteration. Have students hunt for all the words that begin with *s*. (They will find nearly ten in the first two stanzas alone!) Read a stanza or two aloud, emphasizing the sound of each initial *s*, *s*-blend, and *s*-digraph. Lead students to see that when similar sounds are repeated, it gives the language a unified quality. Alliteration can pull a poem together—and make it more fun to read or hear! You can illustrate this point further by pointing out how many tongue-twisters use alliteration: *She sells seashells by the seashore; Peter Piper picked a peck of pickled peppers;* and so on. Then choose an initial letter or sound and make up a tongue-twister of your own!

Following Martin   Level L

Use this poem to introduce internal rhyme. Read aloud the following lines: *To see the parks and pools and schools* and *So Martin grew, and studied, too.* Explain that an internal rhyme consist of words that rhyme within the same line of a poem, rather than words that rhyme at the ends of two different lines. Internal rhymes can add rhythm and musicality to the language. Once students are familiar with the concept, you can help them make up their own poems or sentences containing internal rhymes, for instance: *I met a man who had a van/ He would not stay and drove away!*

The Red Ball   Level L

This work shows students that how a poem *looks* can be just as important as how it sounds or what the words say. A poem's layout can suggest meaning all on its own. Together, study how the poem is formatted. Point out how the shortness of each line makes the poem look longer, which suggests the ball's long path from beginning to end. The lines are also broken in places where the ball's course changes along its journey. The technique is especially evident in lines 4-6: the words *bounced, bounced, bounced* appear right on top of one another, just like a bouncing ball! After exploring these concepts, try creating a visual poem together. You might write a poem about a butterfly, printing the words on a twirly path to imitate its movements. You could also write a poem about ice cream in the shape of an ice cream cone!

A Question of Rhyme   Level L

Use this poem to teach elements of free verse. Explain to students that just because the verse is "free," it still has to be a poem—it is not the same as a story, or any other type of text. Free verse contains different elements of poetry, such as rhythm, alliteration, vivid words, repetition, layout, and so on. Poets don't need to use all of these elements at once; they simply pick and choose the ones that feel right for the subject matter and what they are trying to express. Point out the devices used in this poem: unusual line breaks, interesting layout, two rhyming lines, and repetition. As students become more familiar with these techniques, invite them to write some free verse of their own.

A World of Bugs   Level M

Focus on how visuals can help illustrate the mood of a poem. Reread the first stanza and have students look at the illustration. Ask, "What kind of feeling does the picture give you?" Then read the second stanza as students examine the illustration on the back, and ask the same question. Next, draw students' attention to the title. Ask, "What kind of world does the first page show?" (*unappealing; not a nice place to live*) "What kind of world do you see on the second page?" (*cheerful, a nice place to be*) The illustrations are closely connected to the text: they express exactly what the poem is saying in each part!

Two Words   Level M

Use this poem for a lively game and discussion. Have each student choose two words he or she uses often: they can be as simple as *good morning* or *thank you*, or funny, like the words in the poem (*no way, chill out*). Have students take turns giving clues to their words by listing situations in which they use them. Then have the group try to guess what the words are! Talk about which clues worked best and why; they will probably be the ones that used the most evocative and precise language.

Star Struck   Level M

Focus on this poem's interesting structure. Point out that the words are written like sentences (no capital letter at every beginning line, use of punctuation), but the sentences are written rhythmically like a poem. Discuss how the poet uses line breaks—when a sentence or phrase continues from one line to the next, the reader feels pulled along. If a line break interrupts a sentence in a surprising place, it can highlight a certain phrase or word. In line five of this poem, one sentence ends and a new one begins. Since punctuation provides a natural place to pause, this makes for an interesting effect when read aloud.

Eat the Alphabet   Level M

Focus this lesson on vocabulary and word-play. First, explore the interesting names of the different foods, such as *knish* (the *k* is not silent!), *quince*, and *linguine*. Help students pronounce the words and, if possible, look on the Internet for descriptions of the foods. Next, draw students' attention to the way the poet handles the "X" line of the poem. Say *x* out loud and ask, "What food does that sound like?" (*eggs*) Show students how *X is scrambled X* is a play on *X is scrambled eggs*. Then the poet even refers to his own joke, calling it "awful," but also calling even more attention to the word-play. Discuss why the poet might have used this device: for fun, and probably because there aren't a lot of foods that start with *x*!

What If?   Level N

This work is perfect for writing a parallel poem. A parallel poem follows the same general structure of the original, while being based on a different topic. Reread the poem and discuss how it is composed of various "what if" questions. Its conclusion tells the reader the answer: that if the "what-ifs" came true, the poet would not like it! Encourage students to think of something else that would make the world different, for instance, they might imagine a world where everything were a different color or size, a world where animals could talk, and so on. Have them write a series of questions beginning with "What if," and conclude the poem by telling what their reactions would be!

Lunch   Level N

Use this poem to introduce the concept of irony—expressing what one means by using language that would normally mean the exact opposite, usually for comic effect. Point out examples of irony in the poem by asking questions such as, "Does the character in the poem really think her lunch is 'cool'

compared to her friend's? Would she really rather have cottage cheese than a cupcake?" Then focus on the poem's ironic ending: the character pities her friend for having a "boring" lunch and calls herself a "good friend" for offering to switch! Discuss how the technique adds humor, and then try coming up with a few examples of your own, such as someone describing a car alarm as a "lovely and relaxing sound," or naming a tiny dog "Giant"!

In the Rainforest   Level N

Use this poem to explore mosaic rhymes—when one word with two or more syllables is made to rhyme with two or more separate words. Point out the two mosaic rhymes in the poem: *toucan/you can* and *where it/parrot*. Together, try making up your own mosaic rhymes. You might try starting with words from the poem, for example, *ocelot/toss a lot*, *termite/her might*, or *monkey/one key*!

What Is Pink?   Level N

Some vocabulary in this poem may be difficult for students. Explain words and phrases like *fountain's brink* (the edge of a fountain) and *barley bed* (a spot where barley is planted). This is a good opportunity to discuss the differences between formal and informal English. Some poetry is written in a more casual style, while some works—particularly older ones—are written with more formal, or "fancy," words. Lead students to see that while the vocabulary may be challenging, this kind of language adds a special beauty to the poem.

Mix a Pancake

by Christina Rossetti

Mix a pancake,

Stir a pancake,

Pop it in the pan.

FLIP

Fry the pancake,

Toss the pancake,

Catch it if you can.

Read and Think

1. What does the poem tell you how to do?

2. Which comes first, stirring or frying?

3. When you toss a pancake, it lands on the other side. How do you think doing this helps it to cook?

There Was an Old Woman

A Chinese Rhyme

There was an old woman,

I heard someone tell,

She went to sell pie,

But her pie would not sell.

FLIP

The woman went home

But the step was too high.

She tripped and she fell

And a dog ate her pie!

Leveled Poems for Small-Group Reading Lessons © 2014 by Pamela Chanko, Scholastic Teaching Resources • page 20

Read and Think

1. Did the old woman sell any pie?

2. What did the dog do?

3. How might a high step cause someone to trip and fall?

Six Little Ducks

Adapted Traditional

Six little ducks that I once knew,

Short ones, tall ones, skinny ones, too,

But the one little duck

With the feather in his back,

He led the others

With a "Quack, quack, quack."

FLIP ➤

"Quack, quack, quack.

Quack, quack, quack."

He led the others

With a "Quack, quack, quack."

Leveled Poems for Small-Group Reading Lessons © 2014 by Pamela Chanko, Scholastic Teaching Resources • page 22

Read and Think

1. Name two types of ducks from the poem.

2. How many ducks were there all together?

3. Why do you think a duck's quacking might help other ducks follow him?

I Love Apples!

by Annabel Jane Parker

Juicy apples are so yummy.

How I love them in my tummy!

Ripe and red and tart and sweet,

I love apples! What a treat!

FLIP

When I find one in my lunch,

I take a bite, and it goes

"CRUNCH!"

Read and Think

1. How does the poet feel about apples? Point to the words that tell you.

2. What sound does the apple make?

3. The poet uses the words *juicy, ripe, red, tart,* and *sweet* to describe apples. What other words might describe an apple?

What Is Summer?

by Liam Brewster

Summer is baseball.

Summer is heat.

Summer is ice cream.

Summer's bare feet.

FLIP

Summer is fireworks.

Summer is sports.

Summer is sandy...

And always too short.

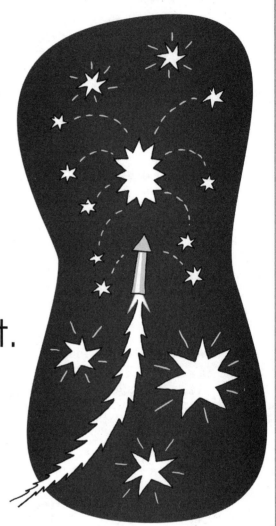

Read and Think

1. What word in the poem describes the weather?

2. What food does the poem mention?

3. Why do you think the poet says that summer is "always too short"? Name some reasons a person would feel that way.

Clouds

by Christina Rossetti

White sheep, white sheep,

On a blue hill,

When the wind stops,

You all stand still.

FLIP

When the wind blows,

You walk away slow.

White sheep, white sheep,

Where do you go?

Read and Think

1. What color is the hill?
2. What happens when the wind blows?
3. How does the title connect to the poem? How are sheep and clouds alike?

Crayons

by Helen H. Moore

I had a box of crayons,

All shiny, straight, and new.

I lent a friend one crayon,

And—oops!—it broke in two!

FLIP ➤

My friend said she was sorry,

But I said, "I don't care."

'Cause now we both can color

With one crayon that we share!

Leveled Poems for Small-Group Reading Lessons © 2014 by Pamela Chanko, Scholastic Teaching Resources • page 30

Read and Think

1. Name two words that describe the crayons.
2. Why did the friend say she was sorry?
3. *Generous* is a word that means "kind and giving." Do you think the owner of the crayons is generous? How can you tell?

But Then

by Aileen Fisher

A tooth fell out

and left a space

so big my tongue

can touch my FACE.

And every time

I smile, I show

a space where some-

thing used to grow.

FLIP

I miss my tooth,

as you may guess,

but then—I have to

brush one less.

Read and Think

1. What happened when the tooth fell out?

2. What shows when the child smiles?

3. What might be a good thing about having one less tooth to brush?

The Child in the Mirror

by Liam Brewster

When I look in the mirror,

Here's what I see:

The one other person

Who looks just like me.

This person is funny.

This person is smart.

This person is friendly,

And has a good heart.

FLIP

This person is someone

I really like seeing,

Because it's a person

I really like being!

Read and Think

1. What does the person see when looking in the mirror?
2. Does the person make others laugh? Point to the word that tells you so.
3. Does the poet think it's a good thing to like yourself? How can you tell?

If You Smile at a Crocodile

by Meish Goldish

The crocodile

Has a toothy smile,

His teeth are sharp and long.

And in the swamp

When he takes a chomp

His bite is quick and strong!

FLIP

So if you smile

At a crocodile,

There's just one thing to say:

If he smiles too,

Be sure that you

Are VERY far away!

Read and Think

1. What are the crocodile's teeth like?
2. Where does the crocodile live?
3. Do you agree with the poet about staying far away from crocodiles? For what reason?

Snowman Song

by Maria Fleming

Sun, sun, go away.

Please don't shine on me today.

Why are you in such a rush

to turn me into sloppy slush?

Sun, sun, can't you see

that your heat is melting me?

Go away sun! Please be nice.

I like being frozen ice.

FLIP ➤

Sun, sun, you're no fun.

I wish I had two legs to run

far, far away from here

before you make me disappear!

Read and Think

1. What is the sun's heat doing to the snowman?

2. Why does the snowman wish he had two legs?

3. How do you think the snowman feels about freezing weather? Can you find a line in the poem that proves your answer?

The Wind

by Holly Gosselin

What happens on a windy day?

Sometimes things just blow away.

On your head, your hat won't stay.

Clouds may seem to dance and play.

Tall, thin trees will bend and sway.

FLIP

The wind is doing its ballet.

Listen, you can hear it say

Whoooooosh…

Whoooooosh…

Whoooooosh…

Read and Think

1. What won't stay on your head on a windy day?

2. What two things do the trees do?

3. A ballet is a kind of dance. Why do you think the poet chose this word to describe what the wind does?

Once There Was a Little Frog

by Annabel Jane Parker

Once there was a little frog

Who sat upon a little log.

When he saw a little flea,

He said, "Hey, there's a treat for me!"

This little flea, he had a hunch,

That he would be the froggie's lunch!

FLIP

The little flea said, "Not today!"

And then he quickly hopped away.

And now there is one hungry frog,

Just sitting on a little log!

Read and Think

1. What is the size of the frog?

2. What did the flea think he would be for the frog?

3. The frog felt hungry when the flea hopped away. How do you think the flea felt? What makes you think so?

The Forgotten Acorn

by Mark Bailey

Look at the squirrels,

They hop all around,

They bury their acorns

Deep under the ground.

They dig up those acorns,

All they can find,

But sometimes an acorn

Can get left behind.

FLIP

From deep underground,

It grows and it grows,

Taller and taller,

And nobody knows

That the beautiful oak tree

On this very spot

Came from an acorn

A squirrel forgot.

Read and Think

1. Name two things the squirrels do.
2. Find the word that describes the oak tree.
3. How does the poet feel about acorns? How does he try to get readers to feel the same way?

Amazing Changes

by Dexter Twisdale

Sitting on a grassy patch

A tiny egg's about to hatch.

Can you guess what will come out

To eat the leaves and crawl about?

A caterpillar, yes, that's right!

It sees a leaf and takes a bite.

FLIP

And then, can you imagine this?

It spins itself a chrysalis!

It sits so still, but by and by

It grows into a butterfly.

So watch and wait, and then one day

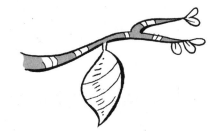

That butterfly will fly away.

Leveled Poems for Small-Group Reading Lessons © 2014 by Pamela Chanko, Scholastic Teaching Resources • page 46

Read and Think

1. What is sitting in the grass?
2. Name something the caterpillar does.
3. *Amazing* means "very surprising." Why do you think the poet used this word in the title of the poem?

Days of Adventures

by Pamela Chanko

Today I saw a dinosaur,

Just walking down the road.

I also saw a princess

As she kissed a tiny toad.

Next, I met an alligator

Crying salty tears.

Later, I'll go back in time

A hundred million years.

Leveled Poems for Small-Group Reading Lessons © 2014 by Pamela Chanko, Scholastic Teaching Resources • page 47

FLIP

Tomorrow I will go to space,

And bounce around the moon.

My picnic with the Queen can wait

'Til Tuesday afternoon.

I know you don't believe me.

I can see it in your look.

But it's true, and you can do it, too…

By opening a book.

····· Read and Think ·····················

1. What is the dinosaur doing?

2. What word describes the alligator's tears?

3. Does the poet think that opening a book can really send someone back in time or into space? What is she trying to say about reading?

A Pet Needs a Vet

by Mark Bailey

Does your puppy have the flu?

Then the vet knows what to do.

Has your kitty hurt her knee?

Then the vet's the one to see.

Has your turtle stubbed his toe?

Then the vet is where to go.

FLIP ➤

Does your pony's voice sound hoarse?

Then the vet can help, of course.

Has your moo-cow lost her moo?

Oh, the vet can cure her, too.

Do you have this many pets?

Maybe *you'll* become a vet!

Read and Think

1. What is wrong with the puppy?
2. Who can cure the cow?
3. Vets are real doctors who cure real animals. That part of the poem is realistic. What are some parts that are *fanciful*, or unrealistic?

My Tree and Me

by Annabel Jane Parker

My tree is my friend,

And here is the reason:

My tree may not talk,

But it tells me the season!

My tree says it's winter

With limbs that are bare.

When its buds start to open,

Then spring's in the air.

FLIP

My tree says it's summer

With fruit that hangs down.

Then it tells me it's autumn

With leaves on the ground.

My tree doesn't speak,

It does not make a sound.

But it still gives me messages

All the year 'round!

Read and Think

1. What happens to the tree in spring?
2. Where are the leaves in autumn?
3. *Limbs* is another word for *branches*. Based on how the branches of many trees look in winter, what do you think *bare* means?

Winter Dress-Up

by Pamela Chanko

At last it is winter! I'm going outside!

I'll glide on the ice and I'll slip and I'll slide.

I'll build a big snowman, taller than tall,

And I won't mind the cold, I won't mind it at all!

But first I have snowboots to put on my feet,

And a warm winter coat to trap in the heat.

Next comes a scarf, wrapped twice around,

And waterproof snowsuit! It's wet on the ground!

After that comes my hat, just like I was told,

And earmuffs, of course, so my ears don't catch cold.

Then come the mittens, to keep my hands warm,

And at last I'm all set for the worst winter storm!

I do love the winter, without any doubt,

But there's so much to do before I go out.

Getting dressed is a game that I can't seem to win.

By the time I am finished, it's time to come in!

Read and Think

1. Name two outdoor activities mentioned in the poem.

2. What does the warm winter coat do?

3. The person in the poem likes winter, but also feels frustrated. Reread the last four lines. What do you think *frustrated* means?

Giant Dinosaurs

by Meish Goldish

Giant dinosaurs roaming around,

Stomping their feet and shaking the ground!

Hungry dinosaurs eating their lunch,

Chewing on a treetop, crunch, crunch, crunch!

Angry dinosaurs having a fight,

Kicking and biting with all their might!

Baby dinosaurs hatching from eggs,

Growing sharp teeth and leathery legs!

FLIP

Playful dinosaurs finding it fun,

Dipping in the lake in the afternoon sun!

Thick-skinned dinosaurs wearing hard scales,

Snapping their heads and giant tails!

Tired-out dinosaurs falling asleep,

Lying on a grass bed, oh so deep!

So many dinosaurs living long ago.

Why did they disappear? No one seems to know!

Read and Think

1. What do the hungry dinosaurs chew on?
2. Where do the tired dinosaurs sleep?
3. *Giant* is a word that means "very, very big." What are some other ways to say *giant*?

Garden Goodies

by Liam Brewster

We're growing a garden

Of good things to eat.

We're growing a garden

Of wonderful treats.

We plant lots of seeds,

And when we are done,

We give them some water

And plenty of sun.

We watch and we wait,

And then what do you know,

Our beautiful garden

Is starting to grow!

FLIP

Potatoes and carrots

Are under the ground,

Tomatoes and cucumbers

Sprout all around.

After we pick them,

They go in a pot.

We cook and we stir

'Til our treat's nice and hot.

Sure, there's vegetable soup

In a can on the shelf,

But it tastes so much better

To grow it yourself!

···· Read and Think ··························

1. What two things do the seeds get?

2. Where do potatoes and carrots grow?

3. Opening a can of soup is much easier than growing all the vegetables yourself. What are some reasons that making fresh or homemade soup might be more fun?

Stormy Weather

by Holly Gosselin

When I hear a pitter-pat
Against my window pane,
I do not frown or mope about,
For I just love the rain!

I rush to put my rain boots on,
My spirits start to soar.
I grab my red umbrella
And go running out the door.

I find a great big puddle
And I jump in with a splatter.
It's muddy and it's very wet.
To me, it doesn't matter!

FLIP

I dance with all the raindrops.

No, I do not mind the storm.

But then I want to go someplace

That's cozy, safe, and warm.

I love the rain, I do! I do!

I never run and hide.

But the best part of a rainy day

Is coming back inside!

Read and Think

1. What sound does the rain make against the window pane?

2. What words describe the puddle?

3. Look closely at the first four lines of the poem. Based on the other words in the text, what do you think it means to "mope about"?

Mamas and Babies

by Dexter Twisdale

Mama ducks have ducklings,

And mama seals have pups.

And joeys will be kangaroos,

Once they're all grown up.

Mama birds have hatchlings,

And horses have their foals.

Mama rabbits nurse their kits

Deep down in rabbit holes.

Leveled Poems for Small-Group Reading Lessons © 2014 by Pamela Chanko, Scholastic Teaching Resources • page 61

FLIP ➤

Mama pigs have piglets.

A cub's a bear-to-be.

When my mama had a baby,

It grew up, and now it's me!

Read and Think

1. What are baby kangaroos called?

2. What do the mama rabbits do, and where do they do it?

3. How does the poet add surprise to the end of the poem? How are the last two lines different from the rest of the poem?

Spring Messages

by Samantha Berger and Pamela Chanko

In April the robin began to sing

To tell the rabbit it was spring.

The rabbit hopped and thumped his feet

To tell the deer the air smelled sweet.

The little deer ran with the bunny

To tell the duck the sky was sunny.

The duck swam off and gave a quack

To tell the cow, "The leaves are back!"

The cow let out a long, deep moo

To tell the horse that flowers grew.

The horse went trotting down the lane

To tell the rooster, "Watch for rain!"

FLIP

The rooster gave a mighty crow

To tell the sheep, "There's no more snow!"

The sheep set off that very day

To tell the goat, "There's lots of hay!"

The goat began to chomp and chew

To tell the dog the sky was blue.

The dog went barking all about

To tell the mouse that seeds would sprout.

The mouse just made a tiny peep

To tell the birds to start to cheep.

Then all the birds began to sing

To tell the bears, "Wake up, it's spring!"

Read and Think

1. What did the duck tell the cow?

2. What happens at the end of the poem?

3. Think about how the poem is organized. How do the poets make each line connect to the next?

Whale Song

by Helen H. Moore

Would you go for a sail

On the back of a whale?

Would you sail through the ocean so blue?

There's a lot you could see

(If the whale would agree),

It's more fun than a trip to the zoo!

FLIP

So please take the chance,

If the chance you should get,

To ride a whale through the ocean.

You'll get mighty wet,

But it's worth it, you bet.

Just be sure to rub on suntan lotion!

····· Read and Think ···

1. What's more fun than a trip to the zoo?

2. What should you put on if you take a ride on a whale?

3. Think about the language and rhythm the poet uses, as well as the advice she gives. Based on these things, how would you describe the poem's tone, or feeling?

Bare Feet and Dog

by Susan Moger

Lovey, my chocolate Lab,

Swims in the creek

Shakes water on my feet

Thumps her tail on my feet

Steps on my feet

Tangles up her leash in my feet

Slurps water from her bowl then

Licks my feet.

FLIP

She has beautiful eyes and a loud bark

She's afraid of thunder but not the dark

Lovey is there for me and always sweet

I love her from my head down to my

sore, wet feet.

Read and Think

1. What breed is the poet's dog?

2. What is Lovey *not* afraid of?

3. Think about why the poet's feet are sore and wet. How does the poem's last line help you understand how much she loves her dog?

Counting Sheep

by Pamela Chanko

When in your bed you cannot sleep,

Whisper rhymes to count some sheep.

One small sheep curls up in bed;

Another rests its sleepy head.

One turns out the bedside light;

Another says, "Goodnight, sleep tight."

One sheep hugs a teddy bear;

Another breathes the cool night air.

FLIP

One sheep sighs a peaceful sigh;

Another hums a lullaby.

One can stay awake no more;

And one last sheep begins to snore.

You've counted sheep from one to ten;

Still awake? Then count again.

But this time, count them in your head—

Don't wake the sheep; they're all in bed!

Read and Think

1. What kind of stuffed animal is one sheep holding?
2. How many sheep are there all together?
3. What about this poem might make the reader feel sleepy? Why?

Leveled Poems for Small-Group Reading Lessons © 2014 by Pamela Chanko, Scholastic Teaching Resources • page 70

Abe Lincoln Grows Up

by Mark Bailey

Once there was a little boy

Who loved to read and write.

His house was made of logs and mud.

He learned by firelight.

The boy grew up to be a man,

And everywhere he went,

The people said, "You're honest, Abe.

You should be president!"

FLIP

And so he was, and what a leader

He turned out to be!

He helped to keep our country whole.

He helped the slaves be free.

Do you love to read and write?

And are you honest, too?

Those things made Abe the president.

Someday it might be you!

Read and Think

1. What was Lincoln's house made of?
2. Name two things that Lincoln did as president.
3. Why might a love for reading and writing help someone become president? Explain your answer.

Stanley the Scaredy-Shark

by Pamela Chanko

Stanley was a scaredy-shark.
The ocean scared him. It was dark!
Stanley found the big blue sea
A deep and spooky place to be.

Seaweed made him quite upset.
It felt so slimy, and so wet!
Seashells made him run and hide.
You never knew who lived inside!

And when an octopus came near,
He hid behind his fins in fear.
When dolphins came to splash and play,
Stanley simply swam away.

FLIP ➡

Stanley was afraid of whales,

And eels and snails and fish with scales.

So everywhere that he would swim,

The animals made fun of him.

But Sam the shrimp, his only friend,

Would stick by Stanley to the end.

So Stanley knew he must be brave

When Sam got trapped inside a wave!

He held his breath and took a dive.

And Stanley got Sam out alive!

And then it spread from sea to shore,

That Stanley was afraid no more!

Leveled Poems for Small-Group Reading Lessons © 2014 by Pamela Chanko, Scholastic Teaching Resources • page 74

Read and Think

1. What did Stanley find upsetting about seaweed? Find the words that tell you.

2. What did Stanley do to prove he was brave?

3. Compare sharks to other ocean animals. Why might people find the idea of a scared shark funny?

Following Martin

by Emma Holzhoy

When Martin was a little boy,

It made him sad and lonely

To see the parks and pools and schools

With signs that said "Whites Only."

He knew he had to change the world,

But had to do it right,

And that meant working peacefully;

No fists would win this fight.

FLIP ▶

So Martin grew, and studied, too,

And came to speak his mind.

He led the march for civil rights

For all of humankind.

Dr. King did change the world,

As hard as that may seem;

But with an open mind and heart

You, too, can live his dream.

Leveled Poems for Small-Group Reading Lessons © 2014 by Pamela Chanko, Scholastic Teaching Resources • page 76

Read and Think

1. What did Martin want to change?

2. According to the poem, what is the right way to make change happen?

3. What does it mean to have an "open mind and heart"? How does this connect to the idea of treating people fairly?

The Red Ball

by Liza Charlesworth

The red ball
slipped from
the baby's hands,
bounced,
bounced,
bounced,
down the cement stairs,
zoomed past
the fire hydrant,
raced through
a championship game
of hopscotch,
crossed the street,
rolled under
a blue car,

FLIP

then zigzagged between

two dozen pairs

of feet,

until one sneaker

kicked it up

into the air

with such force

it landed with a PLUNK!

in the tidy nest

of a jay,

who, by the way,

is still waiting

for the curious thing

to hatch.

Leveled Poems for Small-Group Reading Lessons © 2014 by Pamela Chanko, Scholastic Teaching Resources • page 78

Read and Think

1. What happened to start the ball rolling?

2. Where did the ball go after it crossed the street?

3. The word *curious* has two meanings: it can mean you want to learn more about something, or it can mean that something is unusual or strange. Which meaning does it have in this poem? How do you know?

A Question of Rhyme

by Kathleen M. Hollenbeck

Who says a poem has to rhyme?

It doesn't.

Poetry is words that spill out,

tumbling over each other at first

and then settling into a soothing beat,

    a rhythm you can feel

    from someplace deep inside,

    where your body knows measure and pace and time,

but it doesn't have to rhyme.

FLIP ➤

Poems that don't rhyme can have

words that form pictures,

thoughts that make scenery.

Isn't that poetry?

Isn't that poetry?

That can be poetry

   too.

···· Read and Think ··

1. What do the first two lines of the poem tell the reader?

2. What kinds of words can poetry have?

3. *Beat, rhythm, measure, pace,* and *time* are all words that have to do with music. Why do you think the poet uses them when describing poetry?

Leveled Poems for Small-Group Reading Lessons © 2014 by Pamela Chanko, Scholastic Teaching Resources • page 80

A World of Bugs

by Emma Holzhoy

A bug's an icky, nasty thing.

Mosquitoes bite, and bees can sting.

A picnic doesn't stand a chance

Of being fun when there are ants.

Gnats buzz around and bother you.

Flies don't listen when you "shoo."

If only we could have a day

When all the bugs just went away!

FLIP ➡

But wait a minute, just think twice.

The world would not be half as nice.

For bees make honey, don't you know,

And butterflies help flowers grow.

Ladybugs keep gardens green

By eating pests that can't be seen.

Bugs should never be erased.

They make the world a better place!

Read and Think

1. What do mosquitoes do that is "nasty"?

2. How do ladybugs help gardens?

3. Compare the first half of the poem to the second half. The poet is trying to convince readers of something. What is it? Does she do a good job? Why or why not?

Two Words

by Kathleen M. Hollenbeck

Two words come in handy
each and every day,
rolling off my tongue
as if they're all I have to say.
When I leave my coat at school,
my lunchbox on the bus,
when my homework's missing,
why, I never fret or fuss.

FLIP

When the dog looks hungry

or my clothes are on the floor,

when a frosty winter wind

blows past an open door.

Two small words explain it all.

I say them without thought.

They apply to everything.

What are they?

    I forgot.

Read and Think

1. Name two things in the poem that get left behind.

2. How does the character feel about the two words? What words in the poem make you think that?

3. Some people might describe the character in this poem as irresponsible. Based on the character's actions, what do you think it means to be irresponsible?

Star Struck

by Maria Fleming

When I'm stargazing, I stare and I stare
at all of those sparkly speckles up there.

And I marvel at how every last one
is as big and as bright as our star, the sun—
just farther away. That's why they're so tiny.
If they were closer, they'd be all sun-shiny.

FLIP ▶

And I think as I'm gazing

at all those suns blazing

that stars are

AMAZING.

Read and Think

1. How big and bright are all the stars?

2. What makes them look tiny?

3. Why do you think the poet chose to put the last word on a separate line and print it in all capital letters? What effect does this have on the meaning?

Eat the Alphabet

by Meish Goldish

A is Apple, B is Bean,
C is Celery, fresh and green.

D is Doughnut, E is Egg,
F is Fig, rolling down your leg!

G is Grapefruit, H is Honey,
I is Ice cream, soft and runny.

J is Jello, K is Knish,
L is Lettuce and Lic-o-rice!

M is meatball, N is Nut.
O is Orange, peeled or cut.

P is Pizza, Q is Quince,

R is Rice fit for a prince!

S is Spaghetti, T is Tangerine,

U is Upside-down cake with cream between.

V is Vegetable soup, W is Waffle,

X is scrambled X. (Isn't that joke awful?)

Y is Yogurt, Z is Zucchini,

Let's eat the alphabet on a bed of linguine!

Read and Think

1. What words describe celery?

2. According to the poem, how good is rice?

3. How would the poem be different if it were simply a list of foods in alphabetical order? What makes it more fun to read this way?

What If?

by Helen H. Moore

What if snowballs were hot?

What if water were dry?

What if parrots could swim,

and opossums could fly?

What if:

Teachers were kids;

Doctors never gave shots?

What if:

Cooks put the lids

underneath cooking pots?

What if:

Meanness were nice,

saying "thank you" was rude,

and your parents still thought

you should eat baby food?

FLIP

If all good things were bad,

and all bad things were good,

the world would be different,

it certainly would—

Would you like it?

Not I—

I'd go out of my wits,

If I had to get used

to all these opposites!

Read and Think

1. What question does the poem ask about parrots?

2. Name two sets of words in the poem that are opposites.

3. Based on how the poet describes this different world, what do you think it means to "go out of your wits"?

Lunch

by Pamela Chanko

I am ready for school,
But I have a hunch
That something's not right.
I forgot to pack lunch!

I look in the fridge,
All I see is a peach.
I'll settle for anything
That's within reach.

Oh, there's a pickle,
Some ketchup and mustard,
And isn't that yesterday's
Left over custard?

I search through the cupboards
For anything munchy.
There's uncooked spaghetti!
That sure will be crunchy!

There's a can of green peas,
It will do in a pinch.
Say, packing my lunch
Is really a cinch!

FLIP ▶

At lunchtime I sit
On a bench with my friend,
And look in my bag
At my super-lunch blend.

"I made my own lunch!"
I say with a smile.
"There's enough food in here
For a big crocodile!"

My friend doesn't answer,
Just unpacks his food,
An apple, a cupcake…
Now isn't that rude?

I have such a cool lunch,
Raw spaghetti, canned peas.
Who cares about cupcakes?
I have cottage cheese!

His lunch is so boring!
He takes out a sandwich.
But I'm a good friend,
So I say, "Want to switch?"

Read and Think

1. Is the refrigerator full, or almost empty? What lines in the poem tell you?

2. What happens at lunchtime?

3. How would you describe the personality of the main character in this poem? Find parts of the poem that back up your opinion.

In the Rainforest

by Meish Goldish

Where can you find a toucan?

In the rainforest, you can!

High on a limb is where it

Can be seen with the monkey and parrot.

Squirrels leap from tree to tree,

While bats go flying free.

There's a bee, mosquito, and moth,

Look up! See the hanging sloth!

FLIP

Down on the forest floor

Are big and small creatures galore:

The tapir, snake, and frog,

Plus termites and ants on a log.

Every day, hour by hour,

Butterflies float on a flower.

Colorful lizards also play

In the tall green plants each day.

Ocelots, jaguars, leopards – yes!

The rainforest is a popular address!

Read and Think

1. Name two insects you can find in the rainforest.

2. What word describes the lizards?

3. Do you think the poet would be excited to visit the rainforest? Find reasons in the text that back up your opinion.

What Is Pink?

by Christina Rossetti

What is pink? a rose is pink

By the fountain's brink.

What is red? a poppy's red

In its barley bed.

What is blue? the sky is blue

Where the clouds float through.

What is white? a swan is white

Sailing in the light.

FLIP ➡

What is yellow? pears are yellow,

Rich and ripe and mellow.

What is green? the grass is green,

With small flowers between.

What is violet? clouds are violet

In the summer twilight.

What is orange? why, an orange,

Just an orange!

Read and Think

1. What are two words in the text that describe pears?

2. When are clouds violet, rather than white?

3. The illustrator of this poem didn't include any of the items mentioned in the main text of the poem. What do the illustrations connect to? What question do they help answer?